The Call
of the Wild

JACK LONDON

Saddleback's *Illustrated Classics*™

Three Watson
Irvine, CA 92618-2767
Website: www.sdlback.com

ISBN-13: 978-1-56254-888-9
ISBN-10: 1-56254-888-3
e-book ISBN: 978-1-60291-143-7

Printed in China

Welcome to
Saddleback's *Illustrated Classics*™

We are proud to welcome you to Saddleback's *Illustrated Classics*™. Saddleback's *Illustrated Classics*™ was designed specifically for the classroom to introduce readers to many of the great classics in literature. Each text, written and adapted by teachers and researchers, has been edited using the Dale-Chall vocabulary system. In addition, much time and effort has been spent to ensure that these high-interest stories retain all of the excitement, intrigue, and adventure of the original books.

With these graphically *Illustrated Classics*™, you learn what happens in the story in a number of different ways. One way is by reading the words a character says. Another way is by looking at the drawings of the character. The artist can tell you what kind of person a character is and what he or she is thinking or feeling.

This series will help you to develop confidence and a sense of accomplishment as you finish each novel. The stories in Saddleback's *Illustrated Classics*™ are fun to read. And remember, fun motivates!

Overview

Everyone deserves to read the best literature our language has to offer. Saddleback's *Illustrated Classics*™ was designed to acquaint readers with the most famous stories from the world's greatest authors, while teaching essential skills. You will learn how to:

• Establish a purpose for reading
• Use prior knowledge
• Evaluate your reading
• Listen to the language as it is written
• Extend literary and language appreciation through discussion and
  writing activities

Reading is one of the most important skills you will ever learn. It provides the key to all kinds of information. By reading the *Illustrated Classics*™, you will develop confidence and the self-satisfaction that comes from accomplishment—a solid foundation for any reader.

Step-By-Step

The following is a simple guide to using and enjoying each of your *Illustrated Classics™*. To maximize your use of the learning activities provided, we suggest that you follow these steps:

1. *Listen!* We suggest that you listen to the read-along. (At this time, please ignore the beeps.) You will enjoy this wonderfully dramatized presentation.

2. *Pre-reading Activities.* After listening to the audio presentation, the pre-reading activities in the Activity Book prepare you for reading the story by setting the scene, introducing more difficult vocabulary words, and providing some short exercises.

3. *Reading Activities.* Now turn to the "While you are reading" portion of the Activity Book, which directs you to make a list of story-related facts. Read-along while listening to the audio presentation. (This time pay attention to the beeps, as they indicate when each page should be turned.)

4. *Post-reading Activities.* You have successfully read the story and listened to the audio presentation. Now answer the multiple-choice questions and other activities in the Activity Book.

Remember,

"Today's readers are tomorrow's leaders."

Jack London

Jack London, an American writer of adventure stories, was born in San Francisco, California in 1876. His poverty-stricken childhood taught him many hard lessons.

London quit school at age 14 and worked at a variety of jobs connected with the sea, from stealing oysters to working with the government fish patrol. He went to Japan as a sailor, returned to see the country as a hobo riding freight trains, and was often arrested and jailed.

In 1897 London left for the Klondike—Alaskan gold rush territory. Though he returned penniless, it was a turning point in his life. His experiences there provided the basis for the gripping adventure stories that soon made him a best-selling author. A self-taught writer, London completed nearly 50 novels in 17 years. In them courageous heroes, both animal and human, struggle against the forces of nature and against one another.

Though he became one of this country's most successful and highly-paid writers, London often had financial difficulties, family troubles, and suffered from alcoholism. His death in 1916 is thought to be a suicide.

Saddleback's *Illustrated Classics*™

The Call of the Wild

JACK LONDON

THE MAIN CHARACTERS

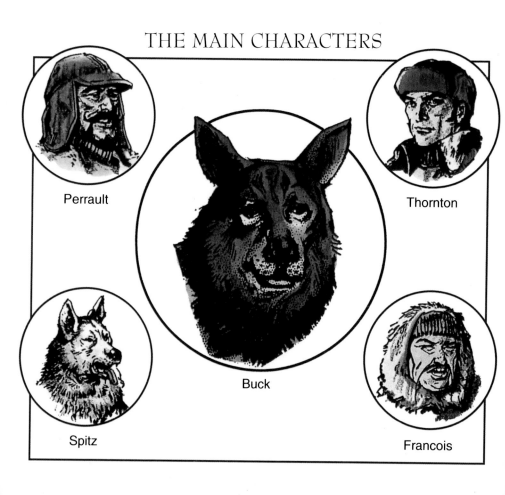

Perrault

Thornton

Buck

Spitz

Francois

Buck was stolen from his peaceful life in the sun-kissed valley of Santa Clara and carried away to the rough northern gold mining country where he had many masters. In the end he would leave the world of humans and become a master himself, a master of the wolves of the wild north country.

Buck was born to an easy life at the home of a wealthy judge in a sunny valley.

Gentle and protective with the Judge's children, Buck walked with his head high among the other animals, for he was king over all things at Judge Miller's.

In the fall of 1897, the Klondike gold strike dragged men from all over the world into the frozen North of Canada. Searching in the Northern darkness for gold, men wanted dogs...heavy dogs with strong muscles for work, and with furry coats for warmth.

I don't care how you get it, but find me a dog! A big one who can work and pull his weight. I'll pay plenty.

Give me part of the money now.

In California, Judge Miller's gardener, Manuel, needed money. He had a wife, many children, and loved to gamble.

When will you bring me the dog?

Tonight. The judge will be away. I'll bring the dog.

At the railroad station....

Buck had let Manuel put on the rope. But when the ends were placed in the stranger's hands, he growled at him.

To Buck's surprise the rope was pulled tight around his neck, choking him.

Angry, he sprang at the man.

But he was met halfway, grabbed by the throat, and thrown over on his back.

The rope tightened cruelly. Buck fought, but his great strength was gone.

He is tiring just in time. Here comes the train.

Buck was thrown into a baggage car and hardly knew he was moving. He was in pain and his throat burned.

Then suddenly, with the uncontrolled anger of a kidnapped king, he sprang for the man.

His jaws closed on the stranger's hand, but the man held on to the rope....

.... and Buck again lost his senses.

What a devil! I'll be lucky if I'm alive to deliver him.

Later, in a shed in the back of a saloon on the San Francisco waterfront, the stranger looked at his damages.

A bloody, crushed hand and my pants ripped from knee to ankle! I got fifty for the job and I wouldn't do it over for a thousand.

Angry and with hurt feelings—Buck began a long trip through many hands.

Watch out for him. He's a killer!

A truck next....

Then a ferry steamer....

....finally two days and nights in a noisy train.

When they took Buck off the train at Seattle, he was an angry beast.

Easy...we don't want this animal breakin' loose!

Buck was taken in the cage to a small yard with a high wall around it. Here he was to meet and learn to fear another man.

Now, you red-eyed devil...come on out!

He came flying out of the cage—140 pounds of anger, headed right for the man who had called him.

Then....

....a terrible whack brought Buck back to the ground.

For the first time in his life Buck had been hit by a club. He did not understand. Again he leaped.

Again he was beaten painfully to the ground.

Now Buck knew it was the club, but he was so mad he couldn't stop. A dozen times, he charged....

....a dozen times the club broke each charge and smashed him down.

For the last time Buck rushed and went down. This time he lay where he had fallen.

He's no easy one at dog-breaking.

Buck knew that he was beaten. He had learned that he stood no chance against a man with a club.

We've had our little battle. Now we can let it go at that. Be a good dog and all will go well.

When the man brought Buck water, he drank eagerly and ate a big meal of raw meat.

Here you are, Buck, my lad!

The club taught Buck a new lesson of life. Life became much harder. He watched other new dogs learn the same lesson.

Then strangers came. Money changed hands, and each time one or more of the dogs was taken away.

They'll do a good job for you!

That big dog! How much?

Three hundred, Perrault. And the Canadian government won't be the loser!

Together with Curly, a good-natured Newfoundland, Buck was led away to the deck of the Narwhal, headed for the frozen North. He said goodbye to the warm Southland.

Buck and Curly were joined by a big snow-white dog from Spitsbergen and a bad tempered dog named Dave. They were cared for by Perrault and a half-breed giant called Francois.

Dave wanted only to be left alone. Spitz was friendly on the surface but sneaky. At the first meal he stole Buck's food.

As Buck ran to punish him, Francois's whip sang through the air, reaching Spitz first.

Spitz, you're a thief!

So Buck found, then and always, that Francois and Perrault were fair men.

After many days, one morning the Narwhal reached land. When the dogs were brought on deck, Buck's feet sank into something white and mushy.

You'll see plenty of snow up here, Buck.

The snow was only the first surprise. Taken from the sunny California countryside and thrown into the wild North country, Buck found each hour filled with surprises.

Curly tried to make friends with a husky dog.

The husky answered her greeting by flashing his teeth and throwing her to the ground.

The watching huskies had waited for this. They closed in and Curly was buried under their bodies.

In two minutes Francois and other men with clubs had chased the dogs, but it was too late for Curly. And Buck had learned a new lesson: Once down, that was the end of you!

These men and these dogs knew only the law of club and teeth. Spitz, watching Curly's death, seemed to laugh, and from that moment, Buck hated him.

Buck's next shock came when Francois put a harness on him, such as he'd seen horses wear at home.

Now, boy, you learn to pull!

Buck had two other teachers. Dave, nipped Buck's hind legs when he was wrong....

....and Spitz, the leader, growled or threw his weight in the tracks to jerk Buck the right way.

Ho, Buck. Stop!

By the time they returned to camp, Buck had made great progress.

That Buck pulls like mad. He learns quick!

That night Buck faced the great problem of sleeping. As a matter of habit, he entered the warm tent.

To his surprise, Perrault and Francois cursed at him and threw pots and pans.

Sacrebleu! No dogs in tent!

Hein! Non, Buck! Out!

Buck walked around the camp and shivered in the icy wind. He wondered where the other dogs were.

Suddenly the snow gave way under his forelegs. He jumped back, afraid.

A friendly bark greeted him. He looked and saw another dog curled under the snow in a snug ball.

So that's the way they did it, Buck thought.

Buck turned 'round and 'round in a big hole in the deep snow.

And so Buck learned another lesson!

Perrault was a messenger for the Canadian government, carrying important information and needed the best dogs. Soon six more were added, and the party was on its way.

Eh, good, nine is enough. Now we head for Dawson!

It was a hard first day's run, up past the timber line, across ice and through deep snow, over the great Chilcoot Divide and down the chain of frozen crater lakes.

Day after day they worked. At night they were starving....

....and tired.

Once when the dangerous rim ice broke away, it was Buck who saved them. As Spitz and the team broke through, Buck pulled backward with all his strength, his front paws on the slippery edge.

By gosh, that Buck has the strength of ten dogs!

A dozen times Perrault, breaking trail, fell through the ice, saved only by the long pole he carried.

At 50° below zero, he was forced to build a fire and dry out or face freezing to death.

You take too many risks! Sometime maybe that pole not long enough!

Spitz knowing Buck could take his place as leader, never lost a chance of showing his teeth. But Buck was too busy learning the new life to pick fights. Though both dogs knew that a fight to the death would happen someday, Buck at first just encouraged the other dogs to turn against Spitz's leadership.

But at one cold, windy camp, Spitz went too far by stealing Buck's covered sleeping spot.

Buck sprang at Spitz and sent him flying, while Francois watched.

Give it to him, Buck ...the dirty thief!

Spitz had been wanting a battle and he watched for a chance to spring. Buck was no less eager, and no less careful....

Suddenly, confusion arose. A pack of starving huskies had broken into the camp.

Sacrebleu! The food!

They're mad dogs!

When the men drove them from the food, they attacked the team dogs.

Spitz charged Buck from the other side. Buck held fast and would not go down...but this was one more mark against Spitz.

At the mouth of the Tahkeena, one night after supper, a snowshoe rabbit sent the whole team off in full cry. A hundred yards away, huskies from a camp of the Northwest Police joined the chase.

Buck led the pack as the rabbit sped down the frozen bed of a creek, but could not gain, the rabbit leaping ahead like some pale ghost.

Spitz left the pack and cut across a bend of the creek.

And before the rabbit could turn, the savage teeth of the Spitsbergen husky flashed and broke its back. As it cried out, the full pack at Buck's heels barked in delight.

Buck, excited by the sight of blood, went for Spitz so hard that he missed the throat.

Spitz, a fighter, who had held his own with all dogs and beaten them from Spitsbergen through the Arctic, and across Canada and the Barrens, got to his feet instantly, slashed Buck down the shoulder and leaped clear.

Buck knew the time had come...it was to the death. The pack drawing up in a circle, their eyes gleaming and their breaths drifting slowly upward, silently waited.

Spitz was a sneaky fighter. He never rushed until he was ready to receive a rush, never attacked till he first defended that attack. He ripped with his teeth and got away, untouched while Buck streamed with blood.

All the while the silent and wolf-like circle waited to finish off the dog that went down.

Buck could fight like all other dogs, but he could use his brain as well. He rushed the big white dog, faking an attack at the shoulder.

....he jumped out of the way at the last moment, his jaws closing on Spitz's left front leg. There was a crunch of breaking bones!

As the white dog faced him fearfully on three legs, Buck drove in again, repeated the trick and broke the right front leg.

Spitz fought madly to keep up even though he was in pain and helpless. He saw the silent circle with shining eyes, hanging tongues and silvery breaths drifting upward. They were closing in on him, as he had seen other circles close in upon beaten dogs in the past.

Only this time he was the one who was beaten. Buck got ready for the final attack, rushed in and out....

The dark circle became a dot on the moon-covered snow....

The next morning Francois discovered Spitz was missing, and Buck was covered with wounds.

That Spitz fight like mad!

Now we make good time. No more Spitz, no more trouble!

What I say? I speak true when I say that Buck two devils!

When Francois linked up the dogs, he brought up Sol-leks as lead dog to take Spitz's place. Buck would have none of it.

Buck drove Sol-leks back, and stood in his place.

Look at that Buck. Him killed Spitz, him think he's to take the job!

Go way, Buck!

Now stay!

But as soon as Francois turned his back....

Okay! I fix you!

When Francois got his club, Buck circled just out of reach. He would accept nothing less than the leadership. He had earned it.

We are late one hour already! Better try it his way....

Okay, Buck, you win!

But Buck was unsure. He knew about clubs. He would not come in until Francois threw it down.

See, Buck, no club. Come on, boy!

He's one smart devil!

Right away Buck took up the duties of leadership, and showed himself to be a better lead dog than Spitz.

Him better even than that old devil Spitz!

Him two devils! Better than one! Him the best I ever see!

The team got back its old-time togetherness. Any member not doing his job of pulling, was soon warned by Buck.

Him taking quick charge now!

They were ahead of the record run. The trail was in excellent condition. In one day they made a sixty-mile dash. Each day for fourteen days, they averaged forty miles. And on the last night of the second week, they topped White Pass and dropped down the sea slope with the lights of Skaguay at their feet.

A record run!

That Buck...him do it! Him worth one thousand dollar, by Gar!

At Skaguay Francois and Perrault were given another job. Francois threw his arms around Buck and wept.

Good-bye, Buck. Never such a dog as you!

And that was the last of Francois and Perrault. Like other men, they passed out of Buck's life for good.

A Scotch half-breed took charge of Buck and his mates. In company with a dozen other dog-teams, they started back over the same old trail to Dawson. It was no light running now, nor record time, but hard work each day, with a heavy load behind, for this was the mail train. It was a dull life, one day just like the other.

Buck did not like it, but he took pride in seeing that his team did a good job.

That Buck, him a tough one!

In camp at night, Buck loved to lie near the fire, eyes watching the flame.

Sometimes he thought of Judge Miller's big house in the sun-kissed Santa Clara Valley.

Sometimes, it seemed the flames were of another fire, and he saw a different kind of man. And beyond that fire were the shining eyes of great beasts.

Dreaming there by the Yukon, these sights and sounds from thousands of years ago would make his hair rise till he cried or growled softly.

It was a hard trip, snowing every day, and hard work wore them down. Since the beginning of winter they had traveled eighteen hundred miles, dragging sleds the whole distance. Buck stood it, keeping the other dogs up to their work and keeping order, though he too was tired.

After 30 days of travel, the team reached Skaguay again. Buck had dropped from 140 pounds to 114 pounds. He and the other dogs were on their last legs.

Poor sore feet, mush on! This is the last. Then we get one bully long rest.

A long rest was needed and expected. But the unexpected happened.

Three days later, Buck watched as he and his team were sold to new owners.

Official orders! the mail must go quick. We got fresh dogs. Sell these ones.

Okay, it's a deal, harness and all.

Buck, that big one, is worth the money alone!

Driven to the camp of the new owners, Buck knew instinctively that these people were out of place in the great Northern adventure.

Oh, what lovely creatures! They'll be such nice pets!

Everything was in disorder. There was a woman, Mercedes, the men called her Charles's wife, and Hal's sister.

How about a hand here, Hal.

Oh, Hal, there are too many clothes for this bag!

Eventually, the sled was awkwardly loaded...with the tent topheavy.

Mush on there, you lazy brutes!

Oh, Hal, don't whip them!

The dogs strained, but they were unable to move the sled.

Precious lot you know about dogs! Lazy brutes, you've got to whip them!

For the dogs' sakes I just want to tell you, you can help by breaking out that sled. It's frozen fast. Throw your weight against the gee-pole and break it out!

Hal broke out the frozen runners and the dogs were able to move the sled.

Ahead, the path turned and sloped steeply into the main street.

As they swung on the turn the sled went over, spilling half its load.

The dogs, angry because of ill treatment and the unjust load, broke into a run. Hal tripped and was pulled off his feet. The dogs dashed on up the street, adding to the gaiety of Skaguay as they scattered the remainder of the outfit.

Kindhearted citizens caught the dogs and gathered the scattered belongings. Also, they gave advice.

Half the load and you might just make it.

Throw away the tent, and all that canned stuff. Somebody would think you were traveling by train.

Late next morning Buck led the team onto the trail. They were starting dead tired and had no heart in their work.

The trip was a disaster. It took these people half the night to pitch camp, and half the morning to break camp. Some days they made only ten miles, some days none at all. Of course they went short on dog food.

You've got to feed these poor dogs more fish!

Mush on, then!

You stupid oaf! You should have brought more!

Buck moved on as in a nightmare. He pulled when he could. When he could not, he fell down and remained till blows drove him to his feet again. Half the dogs died along the way.

Mush! Mush!

It was beautiful spring weather, but neither dogs nor humans were aware of it. The dogs were half dead when they came to John Thornton's camp at the mouth of the White River.

They told us the bottom was dropping out of the trail and we should lay over...but we made it so far!

They told you true. I would not risk myself on that ice for all the gold in Alaska!

All the same, we'll go on to Dawson! Get up, Buck. Mush!

Buck made no effort. He lay where he had fallen. This was the first time he had failed and it drove Hal into madness. He switched from the whip to a club.

Suddenly Thornton sprang upon the man who was using the club.

Buck still would not move. He had made up his mind not to get up. He sensed trouble out there on the thin ice where his master was trying to drive him.

Get up, you lazy animal! I'm in charge!

If you strike that dog again, I'll kill you!

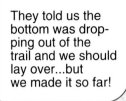

It's my dog! Get out of my way! I'm going to Dawson!

Maybe. Again, maybe not.

Ouch, you....

Thornton picked up Hal's knife himself, and with two strokes cut Buck's harness.

Okay, fella, you're free!

Hal had no fight left in him. In a few minutes the party went on, the remaining dogs limping and staggering. Buck raised his head to see them go.

Suddenly disaster struck! The sled jerked into the air. A scream came back to their ears as the ice gave way. Then a huge hole was all that could be seen. The sled, dogs and people had disappeared below the ice.

Mush on, there, brutes!

Look out... it's breaking!

Time passed...John Thornton was recovering from frozen feet. He and Buck got well together, lying by the river bank through the long, lazy spring days.

Even the dogs, Skeet and Nig, seemed to share Thornton's kindliness. Skeet, while Buck was weak, took over like a mother cat and washed and cleaned Buck's wounds each morning.

Love, real love, entered Buck's life once again. Thornton had saved his life; and he was the ideal master, caring for his dogs as if they were his own children.

For a long time Buck did not like Thornton to get out of his sight. His many masters since he had come into the Northland gave him a fear he would lose still another.

It's okay, Buck, come along. I know what you're thinking.

But in spite of the great love he had for Thornton, the wild animal brought out by the Northland remained alive and active.

He was a thing of the wild, older than the days he had seen and the breaths he had taken. Deep in the forest a call was sounding, making him want to go into the wilderness.

Thornton alone kept him there. When Thornton's partners, Hans and Pete, returned, Buck refused to notice them until he learned they were close to Thornton.

Hi, old partner, did you miss us?

This is Buck, boys. What do you think of him?

I wouldn't want to get into a fight with you while he's around.

By jingo! Not mine-self either!

At Circle City, before the year was out, Pete was proved right. "Black" Burton, a bad-tempered and mean man, picked a quarrel with a newcomer.

I'll beat up on who I please...might as well be you!

This fist is hard as iron. An' when I land it on you....

Take it easy, Burton. He's only a kid.

The men heard something best described as a roar, as Buck leaped for Burton's throat.

Thornton called Buck off. And a miners' meeting agreed that Buck had had reason to fight. Buck's fame and name spread over Alaska.

That fall, while the three partners were taking a boat down a bad stretch of rapids, Buck saved Thornton's life again.

Thornton was flying downstream in a current as fast as a mill-race when Hans stopped too suddenly.

Buck sprang in instantly.

In a mad rush of water three hundred yards downstream he came to Thornton.

Ah, Buck!

When he felt Thornton grasp his tail, Buck swam with all his strength, but it was hopeless.

Can't make it. Current too swift!

From below, the roaring of the falls could be heard. Thornton felt the strong current pull him and knew getting to shore was impossible.

I'll hang on here for a minute. Go back, Buck. Go!

At Thornton's order, Buck swam powerfully for shore. He was dragged from the water just above the point where death became certain.

Grab him, or he's a goner, too.

We've got a chance, Hans, if we can send Buck out with a line!

The line was quickly tied to Buck's neck and shoulders.

Go on, boy, it's all up to you now!

Buck started out bravely but not straight enough into the stream, and the current swept him helplessly past Thornton.

Tough luck, Buck boy!

Hans yanked the rope, and Buck was pulled to the bank more underwater than above.

Though he was half drowned and staggering, Buck raced back up the bank without a command.

Buck dove off the bank as Hans and Pete held the rope.

Buck would not miss a second time.

As Buck reached him, Thornton grasped his shaggy neck.

Strangling, gasping, smashing against rocks and snags, the two were pulled to the bank.

When Thornton came to, he was being rolled over a log by his pals, while Nig was howling over Buck's unconscious body.

How's... Buck?

He's comin' 'round!

Three broken ribs! I'm camping right here till Buck's healed and ready to travel.

No argument there, John! Without Buck, you wouldn't be here!

By yiminey, that is true spoke!

That winter at Dawson, Buck did another bold act that put his name high on the totem pole of Alaskan fame.

Well, I've got a thousand dollars that say he can't and there it is!

You brag about that Buck of yours... but I've got a dog can start a sled with five hundred pounds on it!

Only five? Mine can do seven hundred!

Pooh! Pooh! Buck can start a thousand! And break it out. And walk it a hundred yards!

Well... I... uh....

Thornton's tongue had tricked him. Could Buck pull a thousand pounds? Further he had no thousand dollars. Nor had Hans or Pete. The face of an old friend caught his eye.

I've got a sled outside with twenty, fifty pound sacks of flour on it.

Jim, can you lend me a thousand?

Sure, thoug I don't believe that the beast can do it!

The Eldorado Saloon emptied. Several hundred men banked around the sled to watch the outcome as Thornton knelt beside Buck.

As you love me, Buck! As you love me!

In the sixty-below-zero cold, the sled runners were frozen fast. Not a man in the crowd believed Buck was strong enough to move the sled, normally pulled by ten huskies. The crowd was silent.

Now, Buck. Gee!

A crisp crackling came from under the runners.

The crackling turned into a snapping, the runners slipping to the side. The sled was moving!

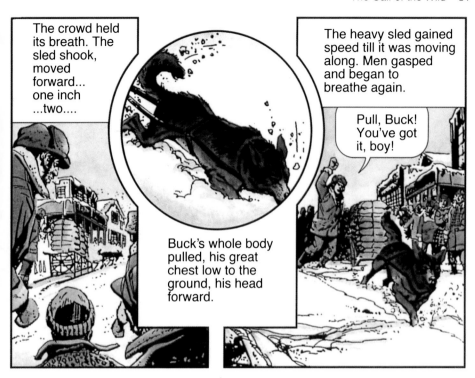

The crowd held its breath. The sled shook, moved forward... one inch ...two....

Buck's whole body pulled, his great chest low to the ground, his head forward.

The heavy sled gained speed till it was moving along. Men gasped and began to breathe again.

Pull, Buck! You've got it, boy!

As Buck neared the end of the hundred yards, a cheer began to grow and grow, which burst into a roar as he passed the mark. Every man was tearing himself loose, even Matthewson. Hats and mittens flew into the air.

Hurray!

He did it!

What an animal!

Buck, old boy... you did it, Buck!

Gad, sir! Gad, sir! I'll give you a thousand for him ...no twelve hundred!

No sir! He's not for sale!

With the money earned by Buck's actions, Thornton and his partners headed into the East after a fabled lost mine.

Nobody living has found the treasure. Might as well be us!

By yingo, yes! They say the nuggets are the purest gold in the Northland!

They lived off the country, Indian fashion, hunting and fishing.

To Buck, these months of roaming about were wonderful.

Summer came, and they rafted across mountain lakes.

Nothing like moose-steak for dinner!

Here's your share, Buck, boy!

This big one's for you, Buck.

No lost mine yet.

But it's a great life!

Spring came on once more, and at the end of their wandering they found, not the lost mine, but a shallow lake in a broad valley.

Look at the gold in that wash pan!

Aye! Like yellow butter!

By yiminey, we stay here now!

Buck at his heels, they crept noiselessly through that other forest.

Each day's hard work earned them thousands of dollars. They packed the gold in moose-hide bags, piling it like firewood outside the log cabin.

It's adding up, boys. Soon we'll be as rich as kings!

With little for the dogs to do, Buck spent hours dreaming by the fire. The dream of the hairy man came to him more frequently.

The hairy man could travel through the trees as well as on the ground.

Often when he dreamed of the hairy man he would also hear a call coming from the forest which filled him with wild hopes. Sometimes he would run to the woods in search of the call as if it were real.

Then one night he heard a real call, clear and sure.

Oww-oooo-ooooo!

He dashed away from the camp, through the woods.

As he drew close he went slowly, carefully....

Ow-oo!

It was a long, lean timber wolf, calling to the sky.

The wolf fled at the sight of Buck.

Buck followed, finally running him into a dead end.

Cornered, the wolf turned, snarling with hair standing on end.

Finally, the wolf seeing Buck meant no harm, sniffed noses with him. They became friendly.

The wolf started off at an easy run, making it clear that Buck was to come. They ran for hours through great stretches of forest, over a dead country across level plains.

Buck was wildly happy. At last he was answering the call, running beside his wild brother. He had done this thing before somewhere in that dimly recalled dream world, running free.

They stopped by a stream to drink, and suddenly Buck remembered Thornton.

Buck turned about and started on the back track. His wild brother howled, but Buck did not look back.

As he got closer to the camp, he sensed danger and continued more slowly.

He followed a fresh trail into a thicket and found Nig's body.

Ahead at the edge of the clearing, he found Hans. Great anger swept over him.

From the camp came the sound of many voices, sing-song sounds that caused Buck to growl with terrible anger. Rushing forward, he saw the Indians dancing about the burning lodge.

For the last time in his life, Buck allowed hatred to overcome his reason. His great love for Thornton caused him to lose all control.

A live hurricane of fury, Buck threw himself at the Indians to kill them all...an animal the Yeehats had never seen before.

There was no holding him back as he attacked them. Their bows and arrows were useless.

Full of terror, the Yeehats fled, crying as they ran that the Evil Spirit was there.

Tired of the fighting, Buck found his way back to the scene of the battle.

It was John Thornton's tracks he was looking for.

He found them near a deep pool, together with a dog's body and the signs of a fight.

The pool, muddy and discolored from the ore boxes, hid what it contained; and it held the body of John Thornton; for Buck followed his tracks into the water from which no tracks led away.

With Thornton dead, Buck did not know what to do. He lay at the pool all day or walked about the camp restlessly.

But, when he looked at the Yeehats' bodies, he felt a great pride...for he had killed man, the greatest animal of all. Even with their weapons they had been no match for him.

That night, again, Buck heard the many-noted call, sounding more real than ever before.

Oww-oooo-ooooo!

And as never before, he was ready to obey. Thornton was dead. The last tie was broken. Man and the claim of man no longer bound him.

Into the clearing the wolf pack came like a silvery flood. Buck, as still as a statue, waited for them.

The pack attacked, backing Buck into the corner of a high bank. Here, so well did he defend his front, that in half an hour, the wolves drew back beaten.

One wolf came slowly forward, and Buck recognized the wild brother with whom he had run. They cried and touched noses.

An old wolf, battle-scarred, came forward to touch noses. Then he sat down, pointed his nose at the moon, and howled. The others sat down and howled. At last, Buck, too, joined in.

Ow-ooo!

Ow-oo!

Soon the Yeehats noted a
change in the breed of wolves.
And they told of a Ghost Dog
that ran at the head of the pack.

Beware! This
one has
cleverness
greater than
ours! He robs
our traps, kills
our dogs, wins
over our bravest
men!

Then the leaders lifted the yelp
of the pack and sprang away
into the woods. The wolves
swung in behind. And Buck ran
with them, side by side with
the wild brother, barking as
he ran.

And when the long winter nights came, the Ghost Dog could be
seen running at the head of the pack through the pale moonlight,
leaping high above his fellows, his great throat a-bellow as he sang
a song of the wilder world, which is the song of the pack.

The
End